Contents

It is one o'clock on a Tuesday afternoon. You have been in court all morning. In one case, your client's only witness is having transportation issues and has not shown up yet. You managed to avoid having the case called until the afternoon, but the judge is not pleased. In a second case, which is being held in a separate courtroom on that same day, you have a trial with a client whom you have just met for the first time and who is facing serious consequences. You have less than an hour over lunch to do legal research in your office, where the voicemails have piled up and a dozen new emails await. You remember that you told another client to swing by the office this afternoon, because you believed you would be done with court by now. As you flip through the mail, you see that you have been appointed to serve as a guardian ad litem (GAL) attorney for a new client in an incompetency matter. The incompetency hearing is scheduled for four weeks from now. You turn to the second page, glance long enough to get a gist of what the case is about, and set the paperwork to the side of your desk. "I'll get to you tomorrow," you think. The next time you pick that paperwork back up will be three weeks from today. You will have less than a week to prepare for court.

    The practice of law can be overwhelming. This is particularly true for attorneys who accept the challenges of appointed work. Resources are limited, and there are times when it can be enough of a struggle to accomplish what you have in front of you that day, to say nothing of working on cases that are set one or two months out. The goal of this series is to identify steps that you as the appointed attorney can take early in the life of a case that will help you hit the ground running. With some effort and planning, and a little practice, these tools will set you up for success down the road. Being a better-prepared attorney not only means a less stressful day at the office but also can mean better outcomes for your clients.

Special thanks to Meredith Smith, Associate Professor of Public Law and Government, for her contributions to this guide.

The Timeline of a Typical Incompetency Case

Incompetency and guardianship cases move fast relative to many other types of cases, making early preparation particularly important. A timeline of key stages is provided below as a guide to your work as a GAL. While not all cases will unfold in the same manner, this timeline depicts the typical course of events and time frames common in incompetency and adult-guardianship cases governed by the North Carolina General Statutes, Chapter 35A (hereinafter G.S.).

Keep in mind that motions in the cause to address any issue pertaining to guardianship can be filed at any time. G.S. 35A-1207.

Figure 1. Key Stages of a Typical Incompetency Case

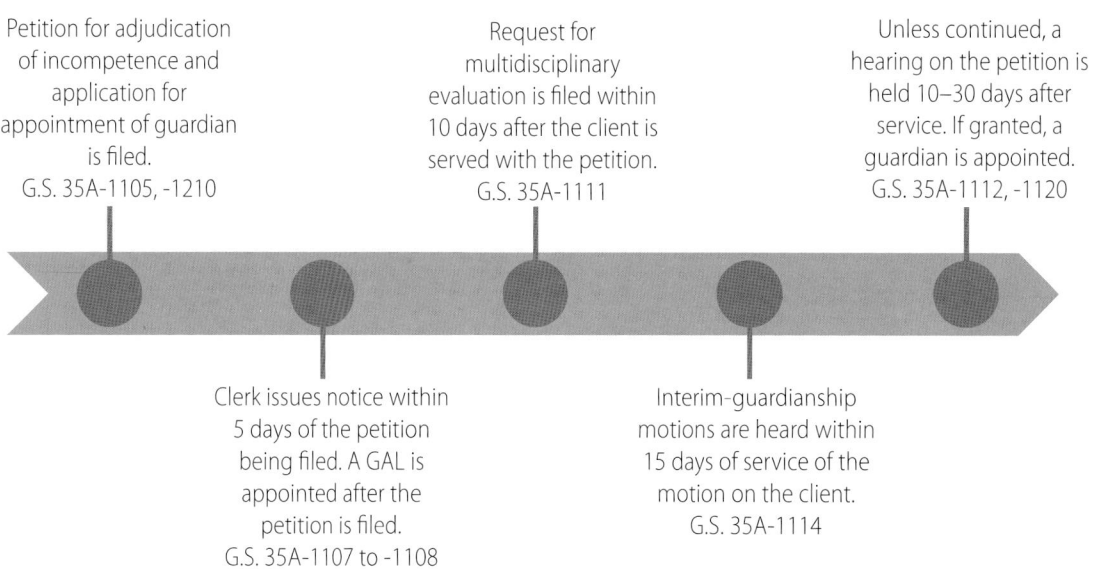

Petition for adjudication of incompetence and application for appointment of guardian is filed.
G.S. 35A-1105, -1210

Request for multidisciplinary evaluation is filed within 10 days after the client is served with the petition.
G.S. 35A-1111

Unless continued, a hearing on the petition is held 10–30 days after service. If granted, a guardian is appointed.
G.S. 35A-1112, -1120

Clerk issues notice within 5 days of the petition being filed. A GAL is appointed after the petition is filed.
G.S. 35A-1107 to -1108

Interim-guardianship motions are heard within 15 days of service of the motion on the client.
G.S. 35A-1114

The First Forty-Eight Hours
Reviewing the Filings

The first thing you should do when you receive a new case appointment is read the entire packet, start to finish.

The Usual Forms

As a GAL in a Chapter 35A case, what are some of the documents you can expect to see when you receive appointment paperwork? If it is a new case, the following should occur:

- You will receive a copy of the *petition for adjudication of incompetence and application for guardian or limited guardian*, typically on N.C. Administrative Office of the Courts (AOC) form AOC-SP-200.
- In some cases, you will receive a *guardianship-capacity questionnaire* that has been completed by the petitioner, typically on AOC form AOC-SP-208.
- You should also receive a copy of the *notice of hearing* on form AOC-SP-201, which serves two major purposes. The notice provides you with the date, time, and location of the hearing, and it serves as the clerk's order appointing you as GAL.

Unlike other types of cases, for example a criminal case, you will *not* find a summons in your packet, as none is issued for an incompetency proceeding.

You may see a *motion in the cause* rather than a petition. If the court previously adjudicated your client incompetent and appointed a guardian to act on your client's behalf, any interested person may file a motion in the cause to request a modification of the guardianship order or to consider any matter pertaining to the guardianship.

The Allegations and Initial Investigation

Take note of what is being alleged about your client. Do the allegations focus on your client's mental or physical needs and issues? Is the nature of the alleged incompetence a lifelong condition, maybe something your client was born with, or does the petition attribute the alleged incompetence to a specific occurrence, such as a traumatic brain injury because of a car accident?

How recently your client allegedly lost capacity may affect how you investigate the case. If it was a recent accident, for example, your investigation will likely include emergency-room records and law enforcement reports, some of which may be incomplete or not yet assembled by their respective agencies. Maybe your client has experienced a slow decline in capacity over time due to a degenerative brain disease, such as dementia. In these cases, you should start thinking about the types of witnesses who may be able to tell you whether they have seen any signs of worsening cognitive skills. You will also want to consider what medical evidence you need to explain your client's prognosis.

Occasionally a petitioner, particularly if that petitioner is a county department of social services, will attach additional documents to the petition to support the allegations. This may include medical, mental-health, or financial records; photographs of your client's home or physical condition; or an opinion letter from a doctor. Take stock of what is included and consider what other information these attachments suggest that you seek out.

The Relief Sought

When reviewing the pleadings, pay attention not just to what is alleged about your client but also to what the petitioner or movant is asking the court to do. If your client is adjudicated incompetent, is the petitioner asking to have a guardian of the estate appointed, a guardian of the person, or a general guardian? The initial filings will also indicate whether the petitioner is asking for a limited guardianship or an interim guardianship. These details tell you what rights of your client are at stake and could affect the types of evidence you gather. While they will give you some indication of how the petitioner sees your client, these details also matter in terms of your timing, meaning how long you have to prepare for a case. An interim guardianship, for example, will typically be heard much sooner than a hearing on a traditional petition.

Review the petition to see who the proposed guardian is. It could be a relative, an unrelated individual, or a disinterested public agent. Part of your dual role as a GAL attorney in an incompetency proceeding is to consider the appropriateness of a possible guardian for your client, to represent your client's position, and to make recommendations accordingly.

Compliance with Procedural Requirements

Your initial review of a case is also a good time to begin ensuring that service and notice requirements have been met. GALs should review the record to determine whether the petitioner has complied with procedural requirements. This review should answer the following questions:

- Has the case been calendared in compliance with the time frames set out in G.S. 35A-1108 for an incompetency adjudication and appointment of guardian, or G.S. 35A-1114(c1) for appointment of an interim guardian?
- Does the paperwork indicate that your client's next of kin have been notified of the petition as required under G.S. 35A-1109? Are there other interested persons who are not next of kin but should be notified because of their relationship or closeness with your client?
- Has your client been served in compliance with G.S. 35A-1109? Your client may not have been served by the time you begin inquiring, but it is good to have this on your radar as the

case unfolds. To verify that your client has been properly served, you will need to check the courthouse file or ask the clerk. Sometimes your client can tell you, or you may observe a copy of the paperwork in your client's house or room at a facility. If service and notice requirements have not been met, consider whether it is appropriate to alert the petitioner and the clerk of that fact, and be prepared to object to a hearing being held before requirements have been satisfied.

Identifying the Players Involved

An important early step is to identify the potential players in the case. Begin by running a conflict check on every person named in the case paperwork. Identifying conflicts of interest early in a case may help you avoid a messier situation later. For example, you would not want to learn the day before the hearing that your client's sister, who is competing with the petitioner for guardianship over your client, was represented by you or your firm in her divorce. The delay that this can cause may be harmful to your client and potentially embarrassing to you for not raising it sooner. An early conflict check will allow for the appointment of a new GAL sooner, if necessary.

Paying close attention to the people involved in a case, not just the parties but any witnesses, service providers, or next of kin who are identified in the filings, will also help you as a GAL begin to think about who you need to talk to in your investigation.

Creating a File

Develop a Filing System

From an office-management standpoint, one of the best things a lawyer can do is to develop a good filing system. There are few feelings worse than being in court, rummaging through a messy folder, and scrambling to find the answer to what should have been a simple question. It is the attorney equivalent of being pulled over and not being able to find your license and registration in your glove compartment. It may seem minor in the grand scheme of things, but an attorney who appears unknowledgeable about a case risks losing the client's confidence and frustrating the judicial official.

Create an Inside-the-Cover Template

One easy way to keep your files organized is to create a template for an inside-the-cover insert for each case. When creating the template, try to think about information that you would like to have quickly available to you for reference. In any court case, this may include party names, dates of birth, addresses, and file numbers. As a GAL in an incompetency case, you also may want case-specific information, like the names of service providers or a list of diagnoses and medications. It may be helpful to designate space in the template for you to quickly record dates, times, and types of work performed, which will make your life easier when submitting a fee application or itemized bill. You can also customize this insert to use as a cheat sheet for an area you may struggle with. For example, you could consider including a simple family tree of your client's relatives if you struggle with name recall or if a case has a confusing familial fact pattern. The appendix includes an example of a template for a Chapter 35A GAL case-file insert. (See page 13.)

Calendar Case Dates

You should add all known dates related to a case to your calendar. Doing so will help you identify possible scheduling conflicts, leaving you ample time to resolve them. Dealing with this ahead of time will save you stress later and will help you avoid delays that may not be in your client's interest.

In addition to adding hearing dates to your calendar, now is also the time to add any self-imposed deadlines or tickler reminders to your calendar. This may include a deadline to issue subpoenas for records or a reminder to follow up with a service provider. The more proactive you are on your end, the more time it leaves for compliance from witnesses and record holders and the less likely their delay will be to harm your client.

Writing a GAL Report

Why a GAL Report Is Important

The statutes do not require a GAL to write and submit a report in an incompetency matter, but some courts do, and many courts allow it even if it is not required. Local practice and requirements may vary, but a GAL should strive to submit a written report before the hearing date. Be sure to serve the petitioner with a copy of your report to give the petitioner an opportunity to respond.

It is often overlooked, but writing a report for the clerk is a key component to serving as a GAL. There are many benefits to writing a report. Writing a high-quality, accurate, and thorough report requires the GAL to have a good grasp of the facts and evidence in a case. It helps you get and stay organized, and it doubles as excellent hearing preparation. A written GAL report is also important information at trial for the clerk and lays the groundwork for what you are ultimately recommending that the clerk do. Often in an incompetency proceeding, the GAL will be the only—or one of the only—hearing participants who is also an officer of the court and whom the clerk is familiar with. A good GAL carries credibility with the clerk, and significant weight may be given to the GAL's perceptions and recommendations in a case. Submitting those perceptions and recommendations in writing is crucial because it lays out the information for the clerk in an organized and helpful way and in a format the clerk can return to as needed.

Submitting a written report has other benefits. It ensures that your report, including your investigative findings and thought processes, are part of the court's file in the event of an appeal. An appeal of a case with no GAL report, particularly if the order is light on specific findings of fact, can leave a gap in the record and be harmful to your client's interests. A written report also serves as documentation of a GAL's work and efforts in a case, which can prove helpful in the event of any allegations that you did not fulfill your responsibilities or as explanation for your fee application.

If for no other reason, a GAL should prepare and submit a written report to the clerk because it is an opportunity to lay out to the presiding judicial official, in an unhurried, prepared, fashion, what you think and why you think it. The GAL report will convey to the clerk what details in a case you want to stress the most, what facts are important, and why you find other details insignificant. The report provides background for the clerk on the players involved, occasionally affecting the weight and credibility the judicial official will give to others in a hearing. Suppose, for example, your client's sister wants to serve as guardian and your client opposes her appointment. During your investigation, you find repeated instances where the sister was dishonest with you, or perhaps with a doctor's office or bank teller. These would be important details for the clerk to learn and might shape the outcome of the case.

If you are not entirely convinced that writing a report as a GAL will make a difference, consider the other areas of your practice, the other courts you appear in, and how quickly you would jump at the opportunity to have a permissible method to provide your narrative of a case to the presiding judge, giving your recommendations for the case and your reasons for feeling that way. Failing to reap this and the other benefits of writing a GAL report is a missed opportunity and potentially a disservice to both you and your client.

Remember that as a GAL, you are both an attorney and a potential witness because of your role in investigating the facts of the case. Your report is a potential area for cross-examination and has the benefit of giving the petitioner an opportunity to understand your views and recommendations.

Why You Should Start Creating the Report Early in the Case

A GAL report necessarily includes information that you as the GAL will learn throughout the life of a case. So why is writing a GAL report listed among the steps you should take during the first few days of receiving a case? Because this is when you should begin working on the report and organizing your notes in preparation for writing the report.

You should create a basic template for a GAL report. As you review the contents of the filings and create your file, take your GAL-report template and plug in the basic case and biographical information, such as file name and number, the date you were appointed, and the date of the hearing. Place a notepad or a few pieces of paper stapled together in your file, and take all of your notes throughout the investigation there. Keeping your records organized and in the same place will save you time when you ultimately write your report and prepare for court. Diligent note taking and organized record keeping will also help you when the time comes to prepare a fee application or billing invoice for your work in a case.

Creating a template for your written reports will help you stay organized and will save you time in each new case. Attached to this guide are examples of GAL report templates for different kinds of cases. These include a report template for a petition for adjudication of incompetence (page 14); a report template for a motion in the cause, including for the modification of guardianship (17); and a report template for when a request for restoration of competency has been filed (19). As shown in the templates, consider including relevant statutory references in your written report. It is good to provide the clerk with the applicable law, and you may also find it serves as a handy cheat sheet for your own use during the hearing.

After drafting reports concurrently with your work in a few cases and fine tuning your templates, you should find that the approach becomes routine and that the benefits become obvious. It is a nice feeling to be a few days out from your hearing and to need only to review or edit your report rather than begin from scratch.

Of course, every case differs. Your template is just that: a basic structure for presenting the pertinent information. What is pertinent and what deserves emphasis necessarily varies. Each report you write should reflect the unique circumstances of the case and your client.

The Next Five Days
Initial Client Contact
Contacting Your Client for the First Time

You should initiate contact with your client within the first few days of being appointed as a GAL. In most appointed cases, that begins with a letter addressed to your client. Do not recreate the wheel with each case. Instead, create a form letter for initial client contact that you can easily update and reuse. A template for an initial-client-contact letter is provided in the appendix (page 21). This letter should explain your role as GAL and what the client needs to do to set up an appointment with you. Sending the letter does not necessarily mean that the client will understand or be able to follow through, and you should not wait too long to see if that happens. Sending the letter does, however, document the beginning of your efforts. Also, the way clients do or do not respond can provide indications of their capacity to manage their own affairs. By sending the letter soon after your appointment, you can afford to wait a few days to see if you get a response before calling or visiting your client yourself (unless you have reason to believe that you need to act sooner).

Prepare for Your Client Interview

Create and use a client-intake template for your initial client interviews. This does not necessarily mean a form for your client to fill out, although that is certainly something you can do if you believe it may be helpful. Using a template to record notes from your introductory client meeting helps ensure that you address the most important matters. Being thorough with your client also stresses the importance of getting firsthand information from your client whenever possible while avoiding the easy trap of putting too much emphasis on what others, particularly the petitioner, allege about your client.

On your template, begin with information that you want to provide to your client. This should include an explanation of your role as GAL, including the duty to determine your client's wishes and to make recommendations regarding the client's best interests. You will also need to explain the nature, purpose, and legal effects of a guardianship proceeding. Discuss your client's rights to contest the petition, to request limits on the guardian's authority, to object to or propose a particular person as guardian, to request a jury trial, and to retain a private attorney. Remind your client of the hearing's scheduled place and time and of your client's right to attend it. If your client needs assistance with getting to the courthouse, you may be able to obtain transportation through the North Carolina Department of Health and Human Services or through your local county department of social services.

Include on your template questions that address common issues in incompetency cases. Examples may include questions designed around orientation (e.g., What is today's date? or Where are we right now?), or information that you can verify with other sources (e.g., How long have you been in this facility?). Incorporate general questions about your client, including questions about your client's personal, professional, familial, and medical background.

When formulating your questions, remember your dual roles as a GAL: to represent your client, which includes determining the client's wishes, and to form a basis for your own recommendations regarding your client's best interests if they differ from the client's wishes. The questions you ask your client should be designed to help you fulfill those purposes. Some of your questions will be intended to gather facts, such as asking how your client is doing, what the client's relationship is like with relatives or caretakers, and what your client needs help with or is concerned about. Other questions may be intended more as a test of your client's memory or capacity. For example, you may want to ask who the client's doctor is or what diagnosis was provided. Asking practical questions, such as what the client would do if there were an emergency, what medications the client takes and when, or what steps the client takes after receiving a bill in the mail, can also be illuminating. Remember to always try to ascertain your client's wishes with respect to finances, health care, residence, employment, visitors, religion, and other major life areas.

Getting a Full and Accurate Picture

It is important to strike a balance in your initial interview between having an idea of what you want to discuss and what you hope to learn from the interview, while also taking the evidence as it comes. You do not want to miss something important because you have blinders on. You will want to provide the clerk with a full picture of your client. Find out who your client is as a person and what your client has seen, done, or experienced that has led to the client's current situation. There is more to your client than capacity alone. What does your client love to do? What about hobbies and interests? Where does your client like to go? Is your client used to being independent? Are your client's current challenges new and unfamiliar? Is your client used to being the one taking care of others? Find out what happened in your client's life that is relevant to the clerk or to a future guardian. The petitioner should not be the only party telling the clerk a narrative. Your interview will help give both you and the clerk a more complete picture of your client's needs.

As a GAL, you may have a client with speech impairments, memory loss, developmental issues, paranoia, or other conditions that affect communication. Remember that your client's ability or willingness to communicate with you may be affected by recent experiences or current surroundings. Your client may be out of a normal routine or away from home. Your client may be in a facility where residents are routinely interviewed by strangers such as doctors, nurses, social workers, or other service providers, and may have interview fatigue. Or it may be more difficult for your client to remember you or distinguish you from other visitors. Your client may be scared or angry and distrustful of others or may be taking new or different medications and still adjusting to the side effects. You will need to take these possibilities into consideration when speaking with your client to be able to put the conversation in perspective.

Moving the Case Forward

Your initial client interview is a good time to take additional steps to put balls in motion and keep the case moving forward while you return to your other cases and clients in the days ahead:

Provide a roadmap. Inform your client how these cases typically unfold and what you generally expect to happen and when. Remember that although you may have been through this process an untold number of times as a GAL, your client has not.

Signing releases. Being a GAL may make accessing some records and information easier, but it may be worth having standard releases prepared ahead of your meeting for your client to review and sign. This may help you avoid future obstacles to obtaining documents. Create a release template for you and your client to write in the names of any providers you identify during your meeting. For some records, your client's release may need language that satisfies the Health Insurance Portability and Accountability Act (HIPAA) or Confidentiality of Substance Use Disorder Patient Records. *See* 45 C.F.R. §§ 160, 164; *See also* 42 C.F.R. § 2.1–.67. Often, these facilities will have their own release templates for your client to sign. If there is a facility in your area that you commonly request records from, such as a hospital or treatment facility, consider making copies of its blank release forms to have readily available for future cases.

Prepare a witness list. Find out who in the client's life has a unique view into the client's daily habits. Include acquaintances and providers who have insight into your client's capabilities or the appropriateness of any potential guardians. Next of kin are provided notice of incompetency hearings and are important to you and your case, but often the person who knows your client best is a neighbor or someone in the community, like a bank teller or pharmacist. Find out whom your client interacts with and why.

Identify alternative placements. Determine where your client wants to live and what alternatives, if any, are agreeable. Ask the client what things are important and what the client's needs are. Ask questions that will help you as the GAL identify important considerations for your client—for example, whether a locked facility is necessary or only an occasional check-in is sufficient. Perhaps your client is fully capable of preparing meals but needs help taking medications. These are important distinctions to make when considering competency and what outcomes are in your client's best interests, including the possibility of a limited guardianship. Remember that there is a statutory preference for in-home placement rather than placement in facilities, and a preference for group or nursing homes over other types of treatment facilities. G.S. 35A-1241(a)(2).

Give the client tasks. Use the initial meeting to establish your client's to-do list. Any task you need your client to accomplish should be addressed at this point to give your client the maximum time possible to complete it. For example, you may want your client to get you a bank statement or a list of current medications. These tasks may look different in an incompetency case compared to other types of cases, given the stronger possibility of your client having difficulty managing affairs. Ask the client to follow up with you at a certain time. Do not rely solely on the client to get you the information, but see whether the client can, which may give you an additional sense of the client's capabilities.

Evidence Gathering and Fact Finding

Other Parties and People, Including Potential Guardians

As a GAL, you will speak to several people other than your client during the life of a case. Typically, this includes the petitioner, the proposed guardian, and your client's next of kin, if any. In some cases, the list may also include social workers, medical and mental-health-treatment providers, and even employers and landlords.

During the first week following your appointment as GAL, begin the process of reaching out to anyone you want to speak with, including people identified during your initial meeting with your client. The way you contact these individuals is a matter of personal preference, but you may find that certain approaches work best, depending on the role that the person has in a case.

For people you are sure you want to speak with, calling and leaving a voicemail explaining why you are contacting them is often the most direct and efficient approach. If there are people you are open to hearing from but whose value to your case is uncertain, such as an estranged aunt or uncle listed in the petition, consider sending them a letter explaining your role in the case and inviting each person to contact you. Doing so helps ensure that these individuals have your information and are at least nominally aware of the situation, allowing them the opportunity to contact you if they have important information to share. If you find yourself in the somewhat uncommon position of believing that meeting with a person without prior notice will be best, make your unannounced visit without writing or calling ahead. In that instance, be sure to identify yourself, your client, and your role in the case.

Contacting the proposed guardian in an incompetency case is of the upmost importance for a GAL, but your initial outreach to that person may differ from how you contact others. If you are appointed sufficiently in advance of a hearing date, consider sending the proposed guardian a letter explaining your role in the case and requesting that the individual contact your office to schedule an appointment. This serves two purposes. First, it helps you get a meeting on the calendar with the proposed guardian. Second, shifting the onus to the proposed guardian to contact you may give you an indication of that person's ability to help manage your client's affairs. If your client's best friend wants to serve as guardian but is unable to respond to an attorney's letter (or follow-up letter, or telephone call), that is concerning. If a proposed guardian schedules a meeting or call, and then fails to follow through, that should be a red flag, particularly if it happens repeatedly or without excuse. Give multiple chances if you can. This is another reason to start this process early so there is time to let it unfold.

Subpoenas and Records Requests

It is inevitable that you will learn of additional people to interview as your work in a case progresses, but you should be able to identify the bulk of the individuals you want to contact from your review of the pleadings and your initial client meeting. Begin preparing a list of anyone who may be a witness, particularly someone who would be testifying as an expert or in a professional capacity. Issuing subpoenas early in the process allows time for service, helps ensure witness availability, and reduces the chance of a potentially harmful delay to your client.

Similarly, as you are reviewing the filings in a new case and speaking with your client, be thinking about what records you would like to see and how they may help you fulfill your GAL duties. Some records may be obvious from the allegations in a petition. With your client's capacity being called into question, mental-health and substance-abuse records are going to be key. If a client has allegedly been hospitalized or financially exploited, seek out the corresponding medical and financial-institution records. Try to think of records of offices or departments that, even if not directly named in the allegations, may shed light on your client or other people involved in the case. Law enforcement may have a history with your client or other people with whom your client has interacted, and that history may document past concerns for maltreatment.

Do not overlook the role that the Department of Social Services (DSS) can play in a case, even when it is not a party to the action. Depending on your client's age, you may want to request records from both child- and adult-protective services related to your client or any proposed guardian. Social-services records can provide a wealth of information. You may need to obtain a court order requiring DSS to provide you with records related to your client. Do not assume that DSS has not investigated allegations involving your client or others important to your case just because it is not the petitioner.

Obtaining these different records from various entities takes time, and the requests do not always look the same. Some record holders will comply with a simple records request written on letterhead explaining your role as GAL. This is another example of a type of letter you can create a template for to save yourself time in future cases. If your client has signed a release for an office to release those records, include a copy of that release with your letter. Other offices will require a subpoena or possibly a court order. Identifying these different record holders (and taking the steps needed to obtain their records) early in a case will help you do your job better. Do not leave yourself stuck between a rock and a hard place by proceeding with a case in which you do not have all the relevant information or seeking a continuance that you may have been able to avoid. Record holders are also more likely to cooperate when given sufficient time to do so. Help yourself avoid the headache of scrambling two days before a hearing and hounding an office for its records.

Background Checks

It is important to conduct background checks on any potential guardian, including any person you or your client plan to propose. This includes both civil and criminal histories.

Often, when DSS is the petitioner, it will pull the criminal background check for the proposed guardian. It is easy for a GAL to get in the habit of assuming that someone else has inquired about a proposed guardian's background. The GAL, however, should be requesting these background checks in any case in which the petitioner does not provide them at the outset. Criminal background checks may tell you something important or disqualifying about an individual, and clerks are going to assume that you have completed those checks. Avoid the nightmare scenario of your client being abused by a guardian after you recommended that guardian's appointment without first running a background check and discovering prior convictions for assault. Keep in mind that certain convictions may prevent the potential guardian from becoming bonded by a licensed bonding company, a prerequisite for serving as a guardian of the estate or general guardian.

Criminal-record checks of different types can be obtained through the clerk of superior court's office and through public-access computers at all courthouses in North Carolina. The procedure for obtaining these records and the associated cost, if any, depends on whether you are requesting a county-only or statewide search and whether you are requesting that the results be certified. For a detailed explanation and links to appropriate forms, visit the North Carolina Judicial Branch's website at https://www.nccourts.gov/help-topics/court-records/criminal-background-check.

Civil background checks should also be completed. A GAL can use the Civil Case Processing System, more commonly referred to as VCAP, to search for any possible red flags in a proposed guardian's background, such as prior restraining orders. VCAP is accessible through the civil department of a clerk's office. For more information on VCAP, visit: https://www.nccourts .gov/services/remote-public-access-program. A VCAP user manual is also available on the state's judicial-branch website at https://www.nccourts.gov/documents/publications/civil-case -processing-system-vcap-user-manual.

For cases where a guardian of the estate or general guardian is being considered, a GAL may want to use VCAP to determine whether there are any existing liens or judgments against the proposed guardian for outstanding debts. Similarly, a GAL may consider using Public Access to Computer Electronic Records, more commonly known as PACER, to find out whether a proposed guardian has filed bankruptcy.

Always remember to check social-media accounts for people involved in guardianship cases, but particularly for anyone who may potentially serve as guardian. Compare what you find on social media to what people tell you in interviews. Social-media histories may be evidence of someone's good and caring nature, or they may make you aware of possible red flags.

Motions

In most guardianship cases, there are no additional filings once the petition is filed and before the hearing on the petition is held. There are times, however, where it may be appropriate for a GAL to file a motion, and you will want to consider that possibility as you begin work in a case. For example, G.S. 35A-1114 specifically authorizes you as GAL to file a motion requesting the clerk to appoint an interim guardian when (1) there is reasonable cause to believe your client is incompetent, (2) there is or reasonably appears to be an imminent risk of harm to your client or your client's estate, and (3) an interim guardian is needed to intervene on your client's behalf before the adjudication hearing.

There may be other motions to consider filing before the adjudication hearing. For example, a GAL may want to consider the appropriateness of requesting a jury trial under G.S. 35A-1110. A client's right to a jury trial is considered waived if a request is not made. Another request for the GAL to consider early in the process is for a multidisciplinary evaluation under G.S. 35A-1111. A motion for a multidisciplinary evaluation must be made in writing within ten days of the client having been served with the underlying petition.

In Summary

No two cases are the same. The work of a GAL will differ depending on the circumstances of each case. There are familiar patterns across cases, however, and steps that are frequently taken. There are steps GALs can and should take in the first week following their appointment that will save time down the road and help you do the best job possible. Some of these steps, such as creating and implementing templates, take time to develop at first. Once you have incorporated them into your routine and become comfortable with using these tools, you should soon see the benefits for you and your clients.

Appendix

Case-File Insert

Key Case Information

File number	
Client's name	
Address	
Telephone	
Date of birth	
Petitioner's name & contact information	
Proposed guardian's name & contact information	
Hearing date(s)	

Client Notes (e.g., diagnoses, medications, service providers)

_____

_____

_____

Quick Time Tracker

Date	Time spent	Work performed

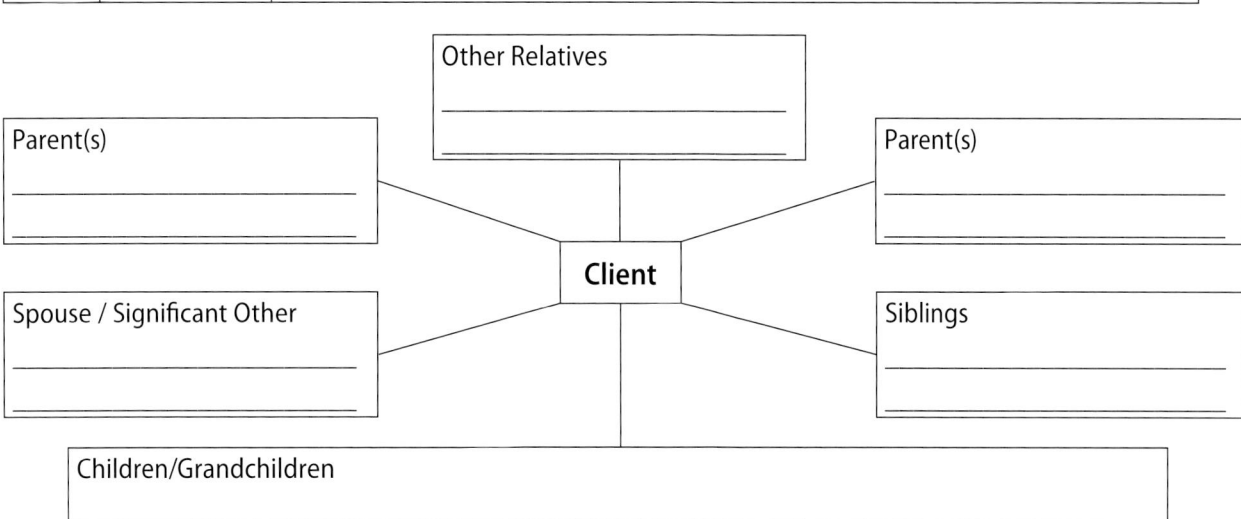

Use this report
template for
cases in which a
new petition for
adjudication of
incompetence
and an application
for appointment
of a guardian has
been filed.

STATE OF NORTH CAROLINA   IN THE GENERAL COURT OF JUSTICE
COUNTY OF COUNTY'S NAME   SUPERIOR COURT DIVISION
                                                                        FILE NO.

IN THE MATTER OF:)
FIRST & LAST NAME   )   *Guardian ad Litem Report*

_____

NOW COMES the duly appointed and undersigned Guardian ad Litem for the Respondent and makes the following report to the Court:

BACKGROUND

1. I, GAL'S NAME, was duly appointed as Guardian ad Litem ("GAL") under N.C.G.S. § 35A-1107 for FIRST AND LAST NAME on DATE OF APPOINTMENT.

2. RESPONDENT'S FIRST AND LAST NAME ("Respondent") is AGE, SEX, AND ADDRESS OF RESPONDENT.

3. On DATE OF FILING, PETITIONER'S FIRST AND LAST NAME ("Petitioner") filed a petition for adjudication of incompetence and application for appointment of a guardian under N.C.G.S. § 35A-1105, -1210. The Petitioner is seeking to have NAME(S) OF POTENTIAL GUARDIAN(S) appointed as GUARDIAN OF THE PERSON / GUARDIAN OF THE ESTATE / GENERAL GUARDIAN for the Respondent.

INVESTIGATION SUMMARY

4. DOCUMENT SUMMARY: Summarize the documents you reviewed as GAL, including medical records, psychological evaluations, law enforcement records, financial statements, and social-services files. Highlight the most important information for the court and detail what conclusions you drew—and want the court to draw—from these documents.

5. INTERVIEW SUMMARY: Summarize the people you interviewed as GAL, including next of kin, friends, neighbors, service providers, and other community members. Describe the key takeaways from those conversations. What did those conversations tell you about your client, your client's competency, and your client's wishes? What do those conversations suggest is in your client's best interests?

6. RESPONDENT-INTERVIEW SUMMARY: Summarize what you concluded from conversations with your client. Share your client's wishes with the court. If you were unable to ascertain your client's wishes, explain why. What should the court know about your client that might not be learned through other evidence?

7. PROPOSED-GUARDIAN SUMMARY: Describe relevant details about the proposed guardian's life, personality, and background. Inform the court of the results of any background checks completed and consider attaching the results to your report. Note any strengths you see in the proposed guardian or any concerns or hesitations you have about their appointment. Inform the court what the proposed guardian and your client's history or relationship has been like.

    a. If you or your client would like the court to consider a different guardianship arrangement than the plan proposed by the petitioner, detail that here. Explain whom you are proposing and why it is in the client's best interests.

APPLICABLE LAW

For items in this section, include only relevant portions. After selecting which citations are applicable, consider adding a brief explanation of why you think it applies to the immediate case. For example, consider summarizing why you think the respondent is competent and the case should be dismissed, or highlight the urgent circumstances that may necessitate an interim-guardian appointment.

8. An incompetent adult is "[a]n adult or emancipated minor who lacks sufficient capacity to manage the adult's own affairs or to make or communicate important decisions concerning the

adult's person, family, or property whether the lack of capacity is due to mental illness, intellectual disability, epilepsy, cerebral palsy, autism, inebriety, senility, disease, injury, or similar cause or condition." N.C.G.S. § 35A-1101(7).

9. A clerk is required to "dismiss the proceeding if the finder of fact, whether the clerk or a jury, does not find the respondent to be incompetent." N.C.G.S. § 35A-1112(c).

10. If the "finder of fact . . . finds by clear, cogent, and convincing evidence that the respondent is incompetent, the clerk shall enter an order adjudicating the respondent incompetent. The clerk may include in the order findings on the nature and extent of the ward's incompetence." N.C.G.S. § 35A-1112(d). In doing so, "the clerk shall either appoint a guardian . . . or, for good cause shown, transfer the proceeding for the appointment of a guardian to any county identified in G.S. 35A-1103." N.C.G.S. § 35A-1112(e).

11. An interim guardian is a guardian "appointed prior to adjudication of incompetence and for a temporary period, for a person who requires immediate intervention to address conditions that constitute imminent or foreseeable risk of harm to the person's physical well-being or to the person's estate." N.C.G.S. § 35A-1101(11).

12. If the clerk "finds that there is reasonable cause to believe that the respondent is incompetent, and: . . . [t]hat the respondent is in a condition that constitutes or reasonably appears to constitute an imminent or foreseeable risk of harm to his physical well-being, and that there is immediate need for a guardian to provide consent or take other steps to protect the respondent[;] or . . . [t]hat there is or reasonably appears to be an imminent or foreseeable risk of harm to the respondent's estate, and that immediate intervention is required in order to protect the respondent's interest, the clerk shall immediately enter an order appointing an interim guardian." N.C.G.S. § 35A-1114(d).

13. A multidisciplinary evaluation is "[a]n evaluation that contains current medical, psychological, and social work evaluations as directed by the clerk and that may include current evaluations by professionals in other disciplines, including without limitation education, vocational rehabilitation, occupational therapy, vocational therapy, psychiatry, speech-and-hearing, and communications disorders. . . . The evaluation shall set forth the nature and extent of the disability and recommend a guardianship plan and program." N.C.G.S. § 35A-1101(14).

14. A multidisciplinary evaluation is considered current if it is not more than a year old at the time it is presented to the court. N.C.G.S. § 35A-1101(14). "If a current multidisciplinary evaluation is not available and the clerk determines that one is necessary, the clerk, on his own motion or the motion of any party, may order that such an evaluation be performed pursuant to G.S. 35A-1111." N.C.G.S. § 35A-1212(b).

15. The "clerk may require a report prepared by a designated agency to evaluate the suitability of a prospective guardian, to include a recommendation as to an appropriate party or parties to serve as guardian, or both, based on the nature and extent of the needed guardianship and the ward's assets, liabilities, and needs." N.C.G.S. § 35A-1212(c).

Based on the above report, the Guardian ad Litem makes the following recommendations to the Court:

For the following recommendations, select only those that are relevant.

ADJUDICATE INCOMPETENT AND APPOINT GUARDIAN:

I.   That the Court find by clear, cogent, and convincing evidence that the Respondent is an incompetent adult under N.C.G.S. § 35A-1101(7).

II. That the Court adjudicate the Respondent as an incompetent adult using the authority granted to the Court under N.C.G.S. § 35A-1112(d).

III. That the Court appoint NAME OF GUARDIAN(S) as the GUARDIAN OF THE PERSON / GUARDIAN OF THE ESTATE / GENERAL GUARDIAN of the Respondent under N.C.G.S. § 35A-1120.

<u>NOT ADJUDICATE AND DISMISS PETITION:</u>

I.   That the Court not find the Respondent incompetent and dismiss the petition under N.C.G.S. § 35A-1112(c).

<u>APPOINT INTERIM GUARDIAN AND/OR ORDER MULTIDISCIPLINARY EVALUATION:</u>

I.   That the Court find that there is reasonable cause to believe that the Respondent is incompetent and that (1) the Respondent is in a condition that constitutes or reasonably appears to constitute an imminent or foreseeable risk of harm to the Respondent's physical well-being and that requires immediate intervention, <u>AND/OR</u> (2) there is or reasonably appears to be an imminent or foreseeable risk of harm to the Respondent's estate that requires immediate intervention in order to protect the Respondent's interests, <u>AND</u> (3) the Respondent needs an interim guardian to be appointed immediately to intervene on the Respondent's behalf before the adjudication hearing.

II.   That the Court appoint an interim guardian under N.C.G.S. § 35A-1114 and specify the interim guardian's powers and duties.

III.   That the Court, using its authority under N.C.G.S. § 35A-1212(b), order a multidisciplinary evaluation of the Respondent be completed, to assist in determining at a later date whether the Respondent is incompetent.

IV.   That the Court urge the interim guardian to consider the Respondent's wishes on matters, as appropriate in the judgment of the interim guardian.

Submitted, this the ____ of _____, 20___.

_____
GAL'S NAME, ATTORNEY
GUARDIAN AD LITEM FOR THE RESPONDENT
GAL ADDRESS AND CONTACT INFORMATION

STATE OF NORTH CAROLINA

COUNTY OF COUNTY'S NAME

IN THE GENERAL COURT OF JUSTICE

SUPERIOR COURT DIVISION

FILE NO.

Use this report template for cases in which a motion in the cause or a motion to modify has been filed.

IN THE MATTER OF:)

FIRST & LAST NAME   )   *Guardian ad Litem Report*

NOW COMES the duly appointed and undersigned Guardian ad Litem for the Ward and makes the following report to the Court:

BACKGROUND

1. I, GAL'S NAME, was duly appointed as Guardian ad Litem ("GAL") under N.C.G.S. § 35A-1107 for FIRST AND LAST NAME on DATE OF APPOINTMENT.

2. WARD'S FIRST AND LAST NAME ("Ward") is AGE, SEX, AND ADDRESS OF WARD.

3. On DATE ORIGINAL PETITION WAS FILED, PETITIONER'S FIRST AND LAST NAME filed a petition for adjudication of incompetence and application for appointment of a guardian under N.C.G.S. § 35A-1105, -1210.

4. On DATE OF ORIGINAL ADJUDICATION, the COUNTY'S NAME County Clerk of Superior Court entered an order adjudicating the Ward incompetent and appointing NAME OF GUARDIAN(S) as the Ward's GUARDIAN OF THE ESTATE / GUARDIAN OF THE PERSON / GENERAL GUARDIAN.

5. Add background information, such as the basis for the court's original ruling or other procedural history, if relevant to the motion now before the court.

6. On DATE OF CURRENT MOTION FILING, FIRST AND LAST NAME OF MOVANT ("Movant") filed a motion in the cause under N.C.G.S. § 35A-1207, seeking DESCRIPTION OF MOTION'S PURPOSE.

INVESTIGATION SUMMARY

7. DOCUMENT SUMMARY: Summarize the documents you reviewed as GAL, including medical records, psychological evaluations, law enforcement records, financial statements, and social-services files. Highlight the most important information for the court and detail what conclusions you drew—and want the court to draw—from these documents.

8. INTERVIEW SUMMARY: Summarize the people you interviewed as GAL, including next of kin, friends, neighbors, service providers, and other community members. Describe the key takeaways from those conversations. What did those conversations tell you about your client, your client's competency, and your client's wishes? What do those conversations suggest is in your client's best interest?

9. WARD-INTERVIEW SUMMARY: Summarize what you concluded from conversations with your client. Share your client's wishes with the court. If you were unable to ascertain your client's wishes, explain why. What should the court know about your client that may not be learned through other evidence?

10. PROPOSED-GUARDIAN SUMMARY, IF RELEVANT: Describe relevant details about the proposed guardian's life, personality, and background. Inform the court the results of any background checks completed and consider attaching the results to your report. Note any strengths you see in the proposed guardian, or any concerns or hesitations you have about their appointment. Inform the court what the proposed guardian and your client's history or relationship has been like.

    a. If you or your client would like the court to consider a different guardianship arrangement than the plan proposed by the movant, detail that here. Explain whom you are proposing and why it is in the client's best interests.

APPLICABLE LAW

For items in this section, include only relevant portions. After selecting which citations are applicable, consider adding a brief explanation of why you think it applies to the immediate case. For example, consider summarizing why you think the clerk should have an agency conduct a report on a prospective guardian, or why the clerk does or does not have grounds to issue an emergency order pending a further hearing.

11. The "clerk may require a report prepared by a designated agency to evaluate the suitability of a prospective guardian, to include a recommendation as to an appropriate party or parties to serve as guardian, or both, based on the nature and extent of the needed guardianship and the ward's assets, liabilities, and needs." N.C.G.S. § 35A-1212(c).

12. If this court finds "reasonable cause to believe that an emergency exists that threatens the physical well-being of the ward or constitutes a risk of substantial injury to the ward's estate, the clerk may enter an appropriate ex parte order to address the emergency pending disposition of the matter at the hearing." N.C.G.S. § 35A-1207(d).

Based on the above report, the Guardian ad Litem makes the following recommendations to the Court:

For the following recommendations, select only those that are relevant:

I. That the Court GRANT the motion in the cause filed by the Movant under N.C.G.S. § 35A-1207. (Add details about what specifically you are recommending the clerk order, such as modifying the type of guardianship, naming who should serve as guardian, or further limiting or adding to the rights and privileges of the Ward.)

II. That the Court DENY the motion in the cause filed by the Movant under N.C.G.S. § 35A-1207. (Add details about what specifically you are recommending the clerk order, if anything.)

Submitted, this the ____ of _____, 20___.

GAL'S NAME, ATTORNEY
GUARDIAN AD LITEM FOR THE WARD
GAL ADDRESS AND CONTACT INFORMATION

STATE OF NORTH CAROLINA
COUNTY OF <u>COUNTY'S NAME</u>

IN THE GENERAL COURT OF JUSTICE
SUPERIOR COURT DIVISION
<u>FILE NO.</u>

Use this report template for cases in which a request for restoration has been filed.

IN THE MATTER OF:)
<u>FIRST & LAST NAME</u>   )

Guardian ad Litem Report

NOW COMES the duly appointed and undersigned Guardian ad Litem for the Ward and makes the following report to the Court:

BACKGROUND

1. I, <u>GAL'S NAME</u>, was duly appointed as Guardian ad Litem ("GAL") under N.C.G.S. § 35A-1130(c) for <u>FIRST AND LAST NAME</u> on <u>DATE OF APPOINTMENT</u>.

2. <u>WARD'S FIRST AND LAST NAME</u> ("Ward") is <u>AGE, SEX, AND ADDRESS OF WARD</u>.

3. On <u>DATE OF FILING</u>, <u>ORIGINAL PETITIONER'S FIRST AND LAST NAME</u> filed a petition for adjudication of incompetence and application for appointment of a guardian under N.C.G.S. § 35A-1105, -1210.

4. On <u>DATE OF ORIGINAL ADJUDICATION</u>, the <u>COUNTY'S NAME</u> County Clerk of Superior Court entered an order adjudicating the Ward incompetent and appointing <u>NAME OF GUARDIAN(S)</u> as the Ward's <u>GUARDIAN OF THE ESTATE / GUARDIAN OF THE PERSON / GENERAL GUARDIAN</u>.

5. Add background information, such as the basis for the court's original ruling or other procedural history, if relevant to the motion now before the court.

6. On <u>DATE OF CURRENT MOTION FOR RESTORATION FILING</u>, <u>MOVANT'S FIRST AND LAST NAME</u> filed a motion in the cause under N.C.G.S. § 35A-1130. In it, this Court is asked to find that the Ward is competent and to enter an order restoring the Ward's competency.

INVESTIGATION SUMMARY

7. <u>DOCUMENT SUMMARY</u>: Summarize the documents you reviewed as GAL, including medical records, psychological evaluations, law enforcement records, financial statements, and social-services files. Highlight the most important information for the court and detail what conclusions you drew—and want the court to draw—from these documents.

8. <u>INTERVIEW SUMMARY</u>: Summarize the people you interviewed as GAL, including next of kin, friends, neighbors, service providers, and other community members. Describe the key takeaways from those conversations. What did those conversations tell you about your client, your client's competency, and your client's wishes? What do those conversations suggest is in your client's best interest?

9. <u>WARD-INTERVIEW SUMMARY</u>: Summarize what you concluded from conversations with your client. Share your client's wishes with the court. If you were unable to ascertain your client's wishes, explain why. What should the court know about your client that might not be learned through other evidence? What does the time you have spent with your client indicate about your client's competency?

APPLICABLE LAW

For items in this section, include only relevant portions. After selecting which citations are applicable, consider adding a brief explanation of why you think it applies to the immediate case. For example, consider summarizing why you think a multidisciplinary evaluation would be beneficial, or highlight the reasons you think the respondent should or should not have competency restored.

10. An incompetent adult is "[a]n adult or emancipated minor who lacks sufficient capacity to manage the adult's own affairs or to make or communicate important decisions concerning the adult's person, family, or property whether the lack of capacity is due to mental illness,

intellectual disability, epilepsy, cerebral palsy, autism, inebriety, senility, disease, injury, or similar cause or condition." N.C.G.S. § 35A-1101(7).

11.   This Court can, on its own motion or the motion of any party, order a multidisciplinary evaluation. N.C.G.S. § 35A-1130(c). A multidisciplinary evaluation is "[a]n evaluation that contains current medical, psychological, and social work evaluations as directed by the clerk and that may include current evaluations by professionals in other disciplines, including without limitation education, vocational rehabilitation, occupational therapy, vocational therapy, psychiatry, speech-and-hearing, and communications disorders. . . . The evaluation shall set forth the nature and extent of the disability and recommend a guardianship plan and program." N.C.G.S. § 35A-1101(14).

12.   A multidisciplinary evaluation is considered current if it is not more than a year old at the time it is presented to the court. N.C.G.S. § 35A-1101(14). "If a current multidisciplinary evaluation is not available and the clerk determines that one is necessary, the clerk, on his own motion or the motion of any party, may order that such an evaluation be performed pursuant to G.S. 35A-1111." N.C.G.S. § 35A-1212(b).

13.   This Court "shall enter an order adjudicating that the ward is restored to competency" if it "finds by a preponderance of the evidence that the ward is competent." N.C.G.S. § 35A-1130(d).

14.   This Court "shall enter an order denying" the request for restoration if it "fails to find that the ward should be restored to competency." N.C.G.S. § 35A-1130(f).

Based on the above report, the Guardian ad Litem makes the following recommendations to the Court:

For the following recommendations, select only those that are relevant:
ADJUDICATE COMPETENT AND RESTORE COMPETENCY:

I.   That the Court find by a preponderance of the evidence that the Ward is a competent person.

II.   That the Court adjudicate the Ward as restored to competency, using the authority granted to the Court under N.C.G.S. § 35A-1130(d).

III.   That in being so restored to competency, the Ward be authorized, under N.C.G.S. § 35A-1130(d), to manage affairs, enter into contracts, control and sell real and personal property, and exercise all rights as if incompetency had never been adjudicated, and that the Division of Motor Vehicles be notified that the Ward is restored to competency. *Id.*

NOT ADJUDICATE COMPETENT AND DISMISS RESTORATION MOTION:

I.   That the Court fail to find by a preponderance of the evidence that the Ward should be restored to competency.

II.   That the Court deny the request for restoration of the Ward's competency, under N.C.G.S. § 35A-1130(f).

ORDER MULTIDISCIPLINARY EVALUATION:

I.   That the Court order a multidisciplinary evaluation of the Ward be completed to assist in determining whether the Ward is competent. N.C.G.S. § 35A-1130(c).

Submitted, this the ____ of _____, 20___ .

_____

GAL'S NAME, ATTORNEY
GUARDIAN AD LITEM FOR THE WARD
GAL ADDRESS AND CONTACT INFORMATION